GOD'S LOVE AND PROMISES:

Bedtime Bible Stories for Young Hearts

Mary Jane Coy

This book is a work of non-fiction. Unless otherwise noted, the author and the publisher make no explicit guarantees as to the accuracy of the information contained in this book and in some cases, names of people and places have been altered to protect their privacy.

WestBow Press books may be ordered through booksellers or by contacting:

WestBow Press
A Division of Thomas Nelson & Zondervan
1663 Liberty Drive
Bloomington, IN 47403
www.westbowpress.com
844-714-3454

Interior Image Credit: Mary Jane Coy, PhD

ISBN: 979-8-3850-0020-3 (sc)
ISBN: 979-8-3850-0021-0 (hc)
ISBN: 979-8-3850-0022-7 (e)

Library of Congress Control Number: 2023910458

Print information available on the last page.

WestBow Press rev. date: 7/10/2023

WESTBOW
PRESS®
A DIVISION OF THOMAS NELSON
& ZONDERVAN

Adam and Eve and the Garden of Eden

Once upon a time, a long time ago when the world was new, there was a beautiful garden called Eden. It was the most wonderful place that anyone had ever seen! It was filled with colorful flowers, tall trees with sweet fruits, and animals of all shapes and sizes. In the middle of the garden, there were two very special people, Adam and Eve. They were the first humans that God created from the clay. He breathed the Holy Spirit into their nostrils, and He loved them very much.

God gave Adam and Eve everything they needed in the garden. He told them they could eat from any tree except one—the tree of the knowledge of good and evil. God warned them that if they ate from that tree, they would surely die.

Adam and Eve were very happy in the garden. They spent their days exploring, tending to the animals, and enjoying the beauty of their surroundings. They were very good at following God's rules and had never disobeyed Him.

One day, a sneaky serpent slithered into the garden and spoke to Eve. The serpent told her that if she ate from the forbidden tree, she would become like God and know everything. Eve was tempted by the serpent's words and decided to consume the fruit from the tree. She then gave some to Adam, who also consumed of the fruit from the tree.

Suddenly, they realized they were naked and felt very ashamed. They knew they had disobeyed God's rule and were afraid of what He would say. They tried to hide from God, but He found them. God was very disappointed in Adam and Eve. He had given them everything they needed, but they had disobeyed His one rule.

God told them that because of their sin, they would no longer be able to live in the garden. They would have to leave and work hard to survive outside the wonderful garden that He had created for them. Adam and Eve were very sad, but they knew they had made a mistake.

God did not abandon Adam and Eve. He provided clothes for them and promised to send a savior who would save them from their sins. Adam and Eve were very grateful for God's mercy and began to live their lives outside the garden.

Adam and Eve's story teaches us that we need to obey God and trust Him. When we do what God tells us, we show Him that we love Him and want to follow Him. But when we disobey, we hurt ourselves and others. We can still ask for God's forgiveness and live according to His will, just like Adam and Eve did.

So as you go to sleep tonight, remember to trust in God, obey His commands, and ask for forgiveness when you make mistakes. He loves you and wants the best for you. May you rest easy, knowing that you are loved and cared for by God. Good night!

Cain and Abel: Learning to Offer Our Best to God

Once upon a time, there were two brothers named Cain and Abel who were born of Eve. Only one wanted to please God. At the time of sacrifice, both offered sacrifices to God. Cain brought some of the fruits of the ground as an offering, while Abel brought the firstborn of his flock and their fat as an offering.

God looked favorably on Abel's offering because he had given his best offering to God, but He did not look favorably on Cain's offering because he had not given of his best as an offering to God. This made Cain very angry, and he became envious of his brother. One day, when they were out in the field, Cain attacked and killed Abel.

God saw what Cain had done and asked him where his brother was. Cain tried to deny what he had done, but God knew the truth. As punishment for his sin, God banished Cain from the land and made him a wanderer.
The story of Cain and Abel teaches us many important lessons. It shows us the importance of offering our best to God and doing so with a pure heart. Abel's offering was accepted because it was the firstborn of his flock and the fat, which were considered to be the best parts. Cain, on the other hand, did not offer his best and did not have a pure heart in his offering.

The story also reminds us of the dangers of envy and anger and from where they stem. Cain's heart was full of envy and anger, which led him to commit a terrible sin, and he suffered the consequences of his actions.

But most importantly, the story of Cain and Abel shows us God's mercy and His willingness to forgive those who repent. Even though Cain sinned, God still showed him mercy and protected him from harm.

Eve had many more children after Cain and Abel, and she became the mother of all living. Through Eve's bloodline, we ultimately trace the lineage of Jesus Christ, who is the source of our salvation and the giver of eternal life. In Jesus Christ, we are made alive, and living in Christ we are united as one family, sharing in the inheritance of God's love and grace.

As you go to sleep tonight, remember the story of Cain and Abel. May it remind you of the importance of offering your best to God, of focusing on God's love from a pure heart, and of seeking His forgiveness and mercy when you make mistakes. Good night!

Enoch: Walking with God

Once upon a time, there was a man named Enoch, who lived a long time ago. Enoch was a good man who loved God very much. He lived in a world where many people did not follow God's ways, but Enoch was different. He walked with God every day and followed His commandments.

Enoch loved to spend time outside, looking up at the stars and watching the birds fly. One day, as he was walking in the fields, he saw a bright light shining in the sky. The light was so bright that Enoch could not see anything else. Suddenly, he heard a voice calling his name. It was God!

God told Enoch that He was pleased with him and that He wanted him to come and live with Him forever. Enoch was so happy to hear this news! He loved God so much and had always wanted to be closer to Him.

So Enoch walked with God and talked with Him every day. He learned more and more about God's love and grace, and he shared this love with others. People would come from far and wide just to hear Enoch speak about God's goodness.

Enoch's love for God was so strong that one day, God took him away to live with Him in heaven. Enoch did not die like other people, but he was taken up to be with God. People were amazed and wondered where Enoch had gone. They searched for him, but he was nowhere to be found.

Many years later, a book called the Bible was written, and Enoch's story was included in it. People learned about his love for God and how he was taken up to heaven. They were inspired by his faith and his willingness to follow God no matter what. Enoch's story teaches us that we can all have a close relationship with God if we choose to follow Him. We can walk with Him every day and talk to Him in prayer. We can also share God's love with others and make a difference in the world.

As you go to sleep tonight, remember Enoch's story and how much God loves you. He wants you to walk with Him and talk with Him every day. He wants you to share His love with others and make a difference in the world. May you rest easy, knowing that you are loved and cared for by God. Good night!

Noah and the Great Flood

Once upon a time, there was a man named Noah who lived in a world that was full of wickedness and sin. People did not follow God's ways, and they did not care about others. But Noah was different. He loved God and tried to do what was right.

One day, God spoke to Noah and told him that He was going to send a great flood to cover the earth. He told Noah to build an ark, a large boat, so that he and his family and many animals could be saved from the flood. God also told Noah to gather enough food and water for them to survive.

Noah obeyed God and started building the ark. He worked hard every day, and people laughed at him and called him crazy. But Noah did not give up. He knew that God had a plan, and he trusted Him.

As the ark was being built, animals started coming to Noah two by two, just as God had said. Noah welcomed them onto the ark, taking care of them and making sure they had enough food and water.

Finally, the ark was finished, and it was time to board. Noah, his family, and all the animals entered the ark, and God closed the door. Then the rain began to fall.

It rained for forty days and forty nights, and the flood covered the entire earth. But Noah and his family were safe inside the ark with all the animals. They ate the food and drank the water that they had gathered, and they trusted in God to protect them.

After the flood had receded, the ark landed on the top of a mountain. Noah sent out a dove to see if the waters had receded, and it returned with an olive branch. Noah knew that the flood was over, and it was safe to leave the ark.

Noah and his family and all the animals left the ark, and they saw a beautiful rainbow in the sky. God had promised that He would never again flood the earth, and the rainbow was a sign of His promise.

From that day on, Noah and his family lived in a new world, one that was full of God's grace and mercy. They knew that God had saved them, and they were grateful.

The story of Noah teaches us that God loves us and wants to protect us, even when things seem impossible. He has a plan for each of our lives, and if we trust in Him and obey His commands, He will take care of us. As you go to sleep tonight, remember the story of Noah and how much God loves you. May you rest easy, knowing that you are safe in His care. Good night!

Abraham and Sarah's Journey of Faith

Once upon a time, there was a man named Abraham and his wife Sarah. They lived in a faraway land, and they loved God very much. One day, God spoke to Abraham and told him to leave his home and go to a new land that He would show him.

Abraham obeyed God, and he and Sarah set out on a long journey. They packed all their belongings and took their animals with them. They did not know where they were going, but they trusted that God would lead them to a good place.

As they traveled, they faced many challenges. They had to cross deserts and climb mountains, and they encountered many strangers along the way. But Abraham and Sarah never lost faith. They knew that God was with them, and they trusted in His plan for their lives.

One day, they arrived in a new land, and God told Abraham that this was the place He had promised him. The land was beautiful with green fields and flowing rivers. Abraham and Sarah were overjoyed and thanked God for His faithfulness.

As time went on, God promised Abraham that he would have many descendants, even though he and Sarah were very old and had no children. They were amazed by this promise and wondered how it could be possible. But they continued to trust in God's plan.

One day, God fulfilled His promise, and Sarah became pregnant. She gave birth to a son, and they named him Isaac. Abraham and Sarah were filled with joy and gratitude, knowing that God had kept His promise. Isaac grew up to be a great man of faith, just like his parents. He continued their legacy, and God blessed him with many children and grandchildren.

God fulfilled His promise, and Abraham became the father of many nations. He multiplied his descendants as the stars of heaven and as the sand upon the seashore.

The story of Abraham and Sarah teaches us about the power of faith and trusting in God's plan for our lives. Like Abraham and Sarah, we may face challenges and difficult times, but if we trust in God, He will always provide for us and lead us to good things.

As you close your eyes tonight, remember the story of Abraham and Sarah's journey of faith. May it inspire you to trust in God and His plan for your life, knowing that He loves you and always has good things planned for you. Good night!

Lot and the Escape from Sodom and Gomorrah

Once upon a time, there was a man named Lot who lived in a city called Sodom. The people of Sodom had become very wicked, and they were doing many things that were displeasing to God.

One day, God sent two angels to visit Sodom and Gomorrah to see if the people there were as wicked as He had heard. When the angels arrived in Sodom, Lot greeted them and invited them to stay with him. Lot was a kind and hospitable man, and he wanted to protect the visitors from the wickedness of the people of Sodom.

However, the people of Sodom soon found out about the visitors, and they surrounded Lot's house, demanding that he give them the men visiting so that they could harm them. But Lot refused, knowing that it was his duty to protect his guests.

As the situation grew more and more dangerous, the angels revealed themselves and told Lot that they had come to destroy the city of Sodom because of its wickedness. The angels urged Lot to gather his family and leave the city before it was too late.

Lot and his family quickly gathered their belongings and fled the city. However, as they were leaving, the angels warned them not to look back. Unfortunately, Lot's wife disobeyed the angels' instructions and looked back to see the city in chaos and ruin, and she became a pillar of salt.

Lot and his two daughters continued their journey and eventually settled in a small town. Even though they had lost everything they'd had in Sodom, they were grateful to be alive and to have each other.

The story of Lot and his family teaches us many important lessons. It reminds us of the importance of hospitality, even when it is difficult or dangerous. It also shows us the consequences of disobedience and the importance of following God's instructions.

Most importantly, the story of Lot and his family reminds us of God's mercy and His willingness to protect those who are faithful to Him. Lot was a righteous man, and he and his family were spared from the destruction of Sodom and Gomorrah because of their faith in God.

As you go to sleep tonight, remember the story of Lot and his family's escape. May it remind you of the importance of faith, obedience, and hospitality, and may it inspire you to follow God's instructions in all that you do. Good night!

Rebekah and the Camels

Once upon a time, there was a man named Abraham who had a son named Isaac. Isaac needed a wife, so Abraham sent his servant to find a wife for him from his own people.

The servant traveled a long way and arrived at a well in a city called Nahor. He prayed to God to show him a sign by having the woman who would be Isaac's wife offer water to him and his camels. Suddenly, a beautiful woman named Rebekah appeared, and she did just that.

Rebekah finished watering the camels and offered the servant water as well. Rebekah also invited the servant to stay at her father's house for the night and offered him food to eat. The servant was amazed by her generosity and knew that she was the one chosen by God to be Isaac's wife.

The servant then gave Rebekah gifts of jewelry and asked about her family, and Rebekah answered that she was the daughter of Bethuel, Abraham's nephew.

The servant told Rebekah's family about Isaac and asked for their permission for Isaac to marry her. They agreed, and Rebekah agreed to marry Isaac, even though she had never met him before.

Rebekah set out on a long journey with the servant and his camels to meet Isaac. Along the way, she learned more about Isaac and his family. She was excited to start a new life with Isaac and to become a part of his family.

Finally, Rebekah arrived at Isaac's home. When Isaac saw her, he knew that she was the one that God had chosen for him. He was overjoyed to marry her.

The story of Rebekah teaches us about the importance of kindness and hospitality. Even though she did not know the servant or his camels, she offered them help and showed them love. She was willing to go on a long journey to start a new life with someone she had never met before because she trusted in God's plan.

The story also reminds us that God has a plan for each of our lives, and sometimes it takes us on unexpected journeys. But if we trust in Him, He will lead us to where we need to be.

As you go to sleep tonight, remember the story of Rebekah and her kindness to the stranger and the camels. May you always trust in God's plan for your life. Good night!

Jacob's Dream

Once upon a time, there was a man named Jacob who lived in the land of Canaan. Jacob was a shepherd, and he had a large family with many sons. One night, Jacob had a very special dream that changed his life forever.

In the dream, Jacob saw a ladder stretching up to heaven with angels going up and down it. At the top of the ladder, Jacob saw God, who spoke to him and promised to bless him and his descendants. God told Jacob that his family would become a great nation and that He would always be with him, protecting him and guiding him.

When Jacob woke up, he knew that the dream was a message from God. He felt grateful and humbled by the promise of blessings and protection. He decided to build an altar at the place where he'd had the dream, and he named it Bethel, which means "house of God."

As time went by, Jacob's family grew, and he had many adventures and challenges. But he always remembered the dream and the promise of God. He continued to live a faithful life, always trusting in God's guidance and protection.

One day, Jacob was presented with a great challenge. He had to face his brother Esau, who he'd had a disagreement with in the past. Jacob was afraid that Esau would seek to harm him and his family. But Jacob remembered the promise of God, and he prayed for protection.

When Jacob finally met Esau, he was surprised to find that his brother had forgiven him and was happy to see him. Jacob was filled with gratitude and relief, and he knew that it was all thanks to God's protection and guidance.

After this event, Jacob's faith in God grew stronger, and he continued to live a faithful life. He had many more adventures and challenges, but he always remembered the dream and the promise of God.

In the end, God changed Jacob's name to Israel, and his sons became the patriarchs of the twelve tribes of Israel. The promise of God came to pass, and his family became a great nation. And all because Jacob had faith in God and trusted in His guidance and protection.

So as you go to sleep tonight, remember the story of Jacob's dream, and always trust in God's guidance and protection. Just like Jacob, if we have faith in God and trust in His plan for us, we, too, can experience great blessings and protection in our lives. Good night!

A Love Worth Waiting For: Jacob and Rachel

Once upon a time, in the land of Canaan, there was a man named Jacob. He was a distant relative of Laban, a wealthy shepherd who had many flocks of sheep and goats.

Jacob had a disagreement with his brother Esau and went to live with Laban. When Jacob arrived in Laban's household, he saw Rachel, Laban's younger daughter, and fell in love with her. Rachel was beautiful, kind, and wise, and Jacob knew that she was the one he wanted to marry.

Laban agreed to let Jacob marry Rachel, but he set a condition: Jacob had to work for him for seven years first. Jacob agreed, and for seven long years, he worked tirelessly for Laban's flocks with Rachel always on his mind.

Finally, the day arrived for Jacob to marry Rachel. He was overjoyed and excited, and he could hardly wait to start his life with her. But Laban had other plans. On the wedding night, he tricked Jacob and married him to Leah, Rachel's older sister, instead.

Jacob was heartbroken and angry, but he did not give up on Rachel. He went to Laban and demanded that he be allowed to marry Rachel, as well, and Laban agreed. But Jacob had to work for another seven years to earn Rachel's hand in marriage.

Jacob's perseverance and commitment to Rachel were tested many times over the years. He faced many challenges, including the difficulty of living in a foreign land with Laban and his family. But Jacob never gave up on his love for Rachel.

Through it all, Jacob trusted in God and in the promise that He had made to him promising to bless him and his descendants. He never lost sight of his dream of marrying Rachel.

Eventually, Jacob and Rachel were married too. Jacob's perseverance and commitment had paid off, and he had finally married the woman he wanted. Jacob, Leah, Rachel, their children, and their animals all traveled back to Jacob's homeland in Canaan.

So as you go to sleep tonight, remember the story of Jacob's perseverance for Rachel. He faced many challenges and obstacles, but he never gave up on his dream of having her as his wife. Just like Jacob, if we remain committed to our goals and trust in God's plan for our lives, we, too, can overcome any challenge and achieve our dreams. Good night!

Joseph's Journey to Egypt

Once upon a time, in a land far away, there was a young boy named Joseph. He had many brothers who loved him very much, but they were envious of him because their father favored Joseph over them. Joseph was also known for his beautiful coat of many colors, which was given to him by his father and made his brothers even more envious.

One day, Joseph had a dream in which he saw himself as a ruler and his brothers bowing down to him. When he told his brothers about the dream, they became even angrier and plotted to get rid of him. So they sold him as a slave to some traders who were passing by.

The traders took Joseph to Egypt, where he was sold to a man named Potiphar, who was a high-ranking official in Pharaoh's court. Joseph worked hard for Potiphar and soon became his trusted servant. But one day, Potiphar's wife tried to seduce Joseph, and when he refused her advances, she accused him of trying to assault her.

Potiphar believed his wife's lies and had Joseph thrown in prison. But even in prison, Joseph did not lose hope. He worked hard and soon gained the trust of the prison warden. Joseph helped the warden manage the prison and became well known among the other prisoners, who included the cupbearer to Pharaoh.

One day, Pharaoh had a dream that troubled him greatly. He wanted to understand what it meant. His advisors were unable to interpret the dream, but then the cupbearer, who had been released from the prison, remembered Joseph and told Pharaoh about his ability to interpret dreams.

Pharaoh sent for Joseph, and he was brought out of prison to interpret the dream. Pharaoh told Joseph about his dream of seven fat cows and seven thin cows, also seven healthy ears of grain and seven withered ears of grain. Joseph interprets the dream for Pharaoh explaining that it meant that there would be seven years of plenty followed by seven years of famine. He also told Pharaoh that he should store up food during the years of plenty so that there would be enough to feed the people during the years of famine.

Pharaoh was very impressed with Joseph's wisdom and put him in charge of storing up the food. Joseph worked hard and was able to store up enough food to feed the people during the years of famine. When the famine came, people from all over the region came to Egypt to buy food from Joseph.

One day, Joseph's brothers came to Egypt to buy food. They did not recognize Joseph, but he recognized them. Joseph forgave his brothers for what they had done to him, but Joseph wanted to test them to see if they had changed their ways. Joseph realized that his youngest brother, Benjamin, was absent. Joseph wanted to see Benjamin very much.

Joseph demanded that his brothers travel back to their father's house and return to Egypt with Benjamin. Once the brothers returned with Benjamin, Joseph welcomed them warmly and provided them with food and provisions. After Joseph was satisfied that his brothers had repented for their past actions, Joseph revealed his identity to them. He told them that he had been sent to Egypt by God to save the people from the famine.

Joseph's brothers were amazed and grateful for his forgiveness. They returned to their father, Jacob, and told him the good news. Jacob did not believe them at first. However, when they showed him the wagons that Joseph had sent to transport him and his family to Egypt, Jacob's spirit revived, and he was overjoyed and grateful.

Pharaoh was also grateful to Joseph for saving the people from the famine, and he made him a high-ranking official in his court. Joseph's journey to Egypt had been difficult, but he never lost faith in God. He had been faithful and obedient to God, and God had blessed him and used him to save many people.

So as you go to sleep tonight, remember the story of Joseph. Even when things are difficult, we must never lose faith in God. We need always trust in God's plan for our lives and be obedient to Him, even when things seem impossible. God can use even the most difficult situations in our lives for good, just as he did with Joseph. Good night!

The Journey of Moses:
From Prince of Egypt to
Leader of God's People

Once upon a time, in a land far away, there was a man named Moses. Moses was born in Egypt during a time when the Pharaoh had ordered all Hebrew baby boys to be killed. His mother, in an act of great courage, put Moses in a basket and set him adrift on the Nile River. The basket was found by Pharaoh's daughter, and having compassion for the baby, she planned to raise Moses as her own.

Moses's sister Miriam followed the basket as it drifted on the Nile River to Pharaoh's daughter. Miriam watched as Pharaoh's daughter drew the basket carrying Moses out of the river. Miriam approached Pharaoh's daughter and convinced her to hire her and Moses's own mother as a nurse, which saved Moses and allowed him to grow up with an awareness of his Hebrew heritage.

As Moses grew, he witnessed the harsh treatment that his people endured as slaves in Egypt. Moses grew to despise the suffering of his fellow Hebrews at the hands of the Egyptians. One day, he saw an Egyptian beating a Hebrew, and in anger, Moses killed the Egyptian. Fearing for his life, Moses fled Egypt and went to live in the land of Midian.

There, Moses married and became a shepherd. One day, while he was tending his sheep, he saw a strange sight. He saw a bush that was on fire, but it was not being consumed by the flames. Moses was curious, so he went closer to the bush to see what was happening.

As he approached the bush, Moses heard a voice calling his name. Moses replied, "Here I am."

The voice said, "Do not come any closer. Take off your sandals for the place where you are standing is holy ground."

Moses was afraid, so he took off his sandals and bowed down before the bush. The voice spoke to him again, "I am the God of your father, the God of Abraham, Isaac, and Jacob." Moses was amazed and afraid at the same time.

God spoke to Moses and told him that He had heard the cries of His people, the Israelites, who were being enslaved by the Egyptians. God had seen their suffering, and He wanted Moses to go back to Egypt and lead His people to freedom.

Moses was afraid and told God that he was not the right person for the job. But God told Moses that He would be with him and would give him the words to say. God also told Moses that He would perform miracles to show the Egyptians that He was the one true God.

Moses still hesitated, so God showed him another sign. God told Moses to throw down his staff, and it turned into a snake. Moses was afraid, but God told him to pick up the snake by the tail, and it turned back into a staff.

God also told Moses that he could put his hand in his cloak and take it out, and it would be leprous. Then he could put it back in his cloak and take it out again, and it would be healed. These signs were to show Moses and the Israelites that God was with him.

Moses finally agreed to go back to Egypt and lead his people to freedom. He met with his brother Aaron, who would help him to speak to the people and to Pharaoh. Moses and Aaron went to Pharaoh and asked him to let the Israelites go free. But Pharaoh refused and made life even harder for the Israelites.

God sent plagues on the Egyptians to show that he was the one true God. The plagues included turning the Nile River into blood, sending frogs, gnats, and flies, killing the livestock, causing boils, hail, locusts, and darkness. Finally, the worst plague of all was the death of the firstborn.

But God had told the Israelites to prepare for this final plague by painting their doorposts with the blood of a lamb. This was to be a sign for the angel of death to "pass over" their homes and spare their firstborns. The Israelites were spared, but the Egyptians were not.

After this final plague, Pharaoh finally relented and allowed the Israelites to leave Egypt. Moses led the people out of Egypt and across the Red Sea with God parting the waters so that they could walk through on dry land. They journeyed for many years in the wilderness with God providing for them by giving them manna to eat and water to drink.

Finally, after many years, they arrived at the land of Canaan, which God had promised to them. Moses died before they could enter the land, but his successor Joshua led them into the Promised Land.

Moses was a great leader who followed God's commands and led his people out of slavery. He was chosen by God to do a great work, and he trusted in God's promises.

Moses is a name with Hebrew origins, and it is derived from the Hebrew word *Moshe,* which means "to draw out." This name is fitting for the story of Moses as he was drawn out of the Nile River as a baby and later drew his people out of slavery in Egypt.

As you go to sleep tonight, remember the story of Moses and how he trusted in God to lead him and his people to freedom. May we also trust in God's guidance and protection in our own lives as well. Good night!

Joshua and the Battle of Jericho

Once upon a time, there was a man named Joshua, who was a faithful servant of God. He had been an assistant to Moses and had helped lead the Israelites out of slavery in Egypt. After Moses passed away, God chose Joshua to be the new leader of the Israelites.

One day, as they prepared to take possession of the Promised Land, Joshua and the Israelite army were on their way to conquer the city of Jericho. As they approached the city, they encountered a man who identified himself as the commander of the army of the Lord. The commander told Joshua to take off his sandals as he was standing on holy ground. Joshua obeyed and listened carefully as the commander gave him instructions on how to conquer Jericho.

The commander told Joshua to march around the city once a day for six days with seven priests carrying trumpets made of rams' horns in front of the Ark of the Covenant. On the seventh day, they were to march around the city seven times, and on the seventh time, the priests were to blow their trumpets and the people were to shout greatly. The commander promised that when they did this, the walls of Jericho would fall down flat.

Joshua and the Israelite army did exactly as the commander had instructed them. They marched around the city once a day for six days, and on the seventh day, they marched around the city seven times. When the priests blew their trumpets and the people shouted, the walls of Jericho did indeed fall down flat, just as the commander had promised.

The Israelites then entered the city and defeated their enemies. But Joshua reminded his people not to take any of the treasures or spoils of war as God had commanded them to consecrate all of Jericho to Him.

Joshua's faith and obedience to God had led to a great victory for the Israelites. He had trusted in God's plan and followed His instructions, even when they seemed strange or difficult. Through Joshua's example, we can learn to trust in God's guidance and obey His commands, even when we don't fully understand why.

As you go to sleep tonight, remember the story of Joshua and the battle of Jericho. May it inspire you to trust in God's plan for your life and to follow His commands, just as Joshua did. Good night!

Printed in the United States
by Baker & Taylor Publisher Services